Contents

About the author

Since graduating from the Royal College of Music and gaining a diploma in Dalcroze Eurhythmics, Ann Bryant has been teaching music, movement and drama. For over twenty years she has specialised in Early Years and Key Stage 1, writing many primary school music resources and leading workshops both in the UK and abroad. During this time Ann has also developed a highly successful career as a children's author, publishing over 110 books in these two distinct fields. Ann is a great believer in the integrated arts. She says, 'I love it when the two sides of my career overlay and overlap, which is why I have so enjoyed producing the four books in the *Start With A Story* series!'

'I used these books with my Nursery and love the way that alongside the fabulous music, drama and dance ideas, all aspects of the Early Years Foundation stage are covered.

The songs were hugely popular, catchy and easy to pick up and we have been introduced to a wide range of musical genres including traditional nursery rhymes, modern action rhymes, classical music, rap and jazz.

The stories in the books are written in a fun way that generates lots of discussion, and having the activities coming out of the story works brilliantly and gave us lots of ideas of our own, too!

But the best thing about the books is that you can use as much or as little as you like, since they are very easy to dip in and out of, so you can pick the bits that best suit you and your class at the time!'

Johanna Scanlon
Head of Nursery

Getting ready to sing – a handy tip
Pretend you are a balloon slowly fizzling as your air goes out. Make a long slow 's' sound as you let your air out and feel your whole upper body caving in. Now *very slowly* uncurl and straighten right up. Then you are ready to start singing.

Introduction

Each of the four books in the series has been specially written with a story as the starting point. The stories are utterly suitable for the Early Years age group, with familiar settings but also opportunities for learning. The books can be used in any order and can be dipped into or worked through. From the story emerge songs, poems and many other music and drama activities which all embrace and help promote the Early Years Foundation Stage curriculum requirements of:

- Personal, social and emotional development

- Communication, language and literacy

- Problem solving, reasoning and numeracy

- Knowledge and understanding of the world

- Physical development

- Creative development.

The story – **A Roaring Success!** – is presented twice in this book. First, we have the whole story. Then, we have each chapter again, alongside a song and a range of music, movement and/or drama activities.

The wonderful musical arrangements on the CD turn every song into a magical adventure. Look out for this logo which shows where there is music for the activities. Even without the book, you are sure to relish the CD!

The activities are set out in chapters like the story itself. Some might act as springboards for other work. Many bear repetition and often benefit from it. The generic ideas which don't particularly relate to music/movement/drama appear in boxes with Daddio to point them out. Feel free to develop the ideas as much or as little as you want. All you need is a space, a selection of percussion instruments and a CD player.

Early Years Settings leaders with no music training will find these books very easy to use. It may be that there are ideas in here which you never realised were musically valid! Specialists will welcome the fresh approach of integrating music with drama, movement and literacy, and highlighting an abundance of cross curricular opportunities.

A Roaring Success!

Chapter 1

A dinosaur popped her head over the top of a mountain. Her name was Gemmasaurus. She narrowed her eyes and stared hard. Was that a little smoke curl she just spotted rising up from the Flames-are-us Mountain opposite? Or did her eyes deceive her?

Alexandersaurus came padding up behind her on his gigantic flat feet.

"Aargh!" screamed Gemmasaurus. "Don't do that Alexander. You made me a jump!"

"Sorry," said Alexandersaurus, in his gravelly whisper. "I can't help being a quiet guy. Anyway, can you see anything?" he added.

"I think I spied smoke!" replied Gemmasaurus.

Alexander craned his long neck. "Smoke means dragons! Hurray! Are we going to scare them?"

"Hang on," Gemma replied. "We've got to wait till I'm quite sure."

On the Flames-are-us Mountain sat a large family of dragons conducting an important meeting.

Every time one of them spoke, a little bit of fire swished into the cold air then disappeared in a flash. Occasionally it left a curl of smoke which rose and rose, growing wispier and wispier.

"What are we going to do about those wicked dinosaurs on Scarytops Mountain?" asked Grandpa Dragon. "I'm fed up with the way they keep charging over here trying to frighten us."

"Me too," said Grandma Dragon. "I'm too old to have to keep watch. I get tired."

Baby Dragon cocked his head. When he spoke, a glittering sparkler came out of his mouth because he was too little to have proper flames. "I don't understand," he squeaked. "Why do we have to keep watch?"

Daddio Dragon reared up on his hind legs. "Haven't you learnt anything, Baby?
We keep watch so that when the dinosaurs come to attack us we can fly up in the air!"

"Yes and scare them back with our fire and our shrieks!" added Bigboy Dragon, grinning his head off.

"Why?" asked Baby simply.

"Because!" said Bigboy.

"Oh," said Baby, wearing a puzzled frown.

Chapter 2

On Scarytops Mountain the dinosaurs were preparing for battle. How they beamed. They loved charging into the valley and up the Flames-are-us Mountain opposite.

"Show us your claws, Luca!" some of the young dinosaurs cried. "Let's see if they've grown!"

Lucasaurus smiled round proudly. "Yes, they're over half a metre long now. Bigger than a garden rake!"

The young dinosaurs turned to Annasaurus. "Give us a growl, Anna!"

Then everyone shivered and clung to each other because when Annasaurus growled the whole mountain shook.

"Those dragons are going to be terrified!" giggled Gemmasauras.

"Yes, but don't growl until we've got right up to them!" Christophersaurus said in a bit of a bossy voice. "You're always giving the game away, Anna!"

"Sorry," said Annasaurus. I just can't help myself!"

"OK, time for the pre-battle chant," announced Sebasaurus. "Gather round on the campus, everyone!"

There was a great deal of shuffling into position and when all the dinosaurs had formed a neat circle, Seb stood tall in the middle, his long neck stretched upward, his head flung back to the dark sky, and cried, "Let the chanting begin! One two THREE...!"

We're off to scare the dragons
We're off to scare the dragons
We're off to scare the dragons into the air
To give them a *fright!*

We're off to scare the dragons
We're off to scare the dragons
We're off to scare the dragons into the air
To *night!*

We're off to scare the dragons
We're off to scare the dragons
We're off to scare the dragons into the air
That's right!

Chapter 3

"Who's on guard tonight?" asked Biggirl Dragon.

"Me," replied Auntie Dragon. "Worst luck," she added under her fiery breath.

"Don't fall asleep whatever you do!" said Uncle Dragon.

So whilst all the dragons found themselves cosy spots to snuggle into for a good night's sleep, Auntie Dragon sat right at the top of the Flames-are-us Mountain and looked up at the sky. There was only one star shining and she started to imagine what its name might be. "I know," she said to herself, "I'll try to think of star names beginning with every letter of the alphabet. That will keep me awake." So she did. But she'd only got as far as G for Gorgonzola when her eyelids started to droop, then her head began to loll, and after a few seconds, from her half open mouth came a loud snoring that echoed right down the valley.

The dinosaurs had to stifle their giggles as they crept through the valley towards the Flames-are-us Mountain. They were only half way up, however, when the beautiful peace of the night was suddenly shattered by the most almighty roar.

"Sorry everyone!" wailed Annasaurus a second later. "I couldn't help it. It just slipped out!"

"You silly creature!" shouted Christophersaurus as there came a different kind of roar from the Flames-are-us Mountain — the roar of fire erupting from the nostrils of the dragons. And next minute there was a violent beating and flapping of wings as the whole family rose into the air.

"Well done, Auntie!" cried Daddio Dragon enthusiastically. "I never knew you could roar such a loud warning!" Then he flew down towards the dinosaurs calling, "You'll never catch us. We're cleverer by far than you!"

The dinosaurs thought they would look rather foolish if they admitted it had been one of them who had roared, so they just leapt off in enormous bounds, growling, "We'll get you one of these days! You just wait!"

But little Ellenasaurus was falling behind because of her unusually short legs and in the end Clarasaurus had to scoop her up and run along carrying her.

All in all it was a big relief to get home.

Chapter 4

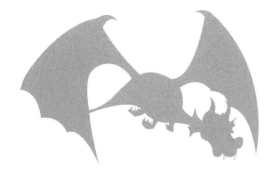

"I'm not putting up with those dinosaur bullies for
another second!" declared Grandma Dragon.
"We need to teach them a lesson!"

"Quite agree!" nodded the others.

"Let's fly around their mountain singing songs and blowing out smoke to make
them cough and keep them awake all night!" suggested Littleboy Dragon.

"Can I just stay here?" asked Baby Dragon.

"Absolutely not!" Daddio replied. "You are quite old enough to join in."

So that night, the dragons waited until it was completely dark and then they silently rose into the air and swooped off
towards Scarytops Mountain. But when they were scarcely over the valley that separated the two mountains, there
came a sharp whip of lightning that lit up the sky, followed by a deep bass drum roll of thunder.

"Keep going!" commanded Daddio. "The rain won't start for a few minutes. We've still got time to scare the living
daylights out of them!"

"Don't be silly, Daddio!" said Mumma Dragon. "What's the point? You know our fire will be put out if it rains. Let's just
go home."

"We're almost there!" said Daddio. "Come on everyone. Why let a bit of rain put you off!" Then as he swooped over
Scarytops Mountain, he opened his mouth and let out a great ball of bright amber fire.

At that very moment the clouds above crashed against each other, and down came lashing needles of rain.
Daddio tried to let out another burst of fire but it was no good. The moment the rain hit his flames, they fizzled
into nothingness.

"Ha ha!" laughed the dinosaurs, looking up at the soaking wet dragons.
"You've lost your fire! Serves you right!"

"Come on!" cried Uncle Dragon. "Let's get back.
We're getting soaked. Hurry! Hurry!"

"Shelter in caves!" called Grandpa Dragon, flying very high so that his
enormous wings would protect the smaller dragons from the rain.

And all this time not one single one of the dragons had noticed that someone
was missing. Poor little Baby Dragon had been left behind because he didn't
have any flap left in his wings, nor any squeak in his voice to call out. So he
just lay down on Scarytops Mountain in the middle of all the Dinosaurs.

Chapter 5

The dragons couldn't wait to get out of the rain. They plunged into an enormous dark cavern where their eyes glinted and glimmered in the blackness.

"That was rubbish!" said Littleboy Dragon. "I hate the rain!"

"Me too!" Littlegirl Dragon agreed.

"Never mind that," said Daddio a bit grumpily. "We need to make a plan to pay those dinosaurs back. I can't stand it when they laugh at us!"

"As soon as this horrible rain stops we should fly back over there," suggested Bigboy Dragon. "They certainly won't be expecting us so soon."

"Baby Dragon will be too tired for that," pointed out Mumma Dragon. Then she suddenly stood on her hind legs and whipped her head from side to side, trying to see in the dim light of the cave. "Where are you, Baby Dragon?" she called, her voice echoing round the cavern.

For a few moments a wondering silence fell over the dragons and nothing could be seen but darting, flicking eyes. Then Bigboy Dragon spoke. "Don't worry about Baby. He's always wandering off. He'll be somewhere around."

"I'm going to look for him," said Mumma Dragon. And off she went.

Meanwhile Clarasaurus was bending over Baby Dragon. She wasn't sure what to say. But someone had to say something. The other dinosaurs were just staring at Baby as though he was an alien.

... hadn't you better go and find your family?" mumbled Clarasaurus eventually.

"I ... I can't," Baby Dragon said in a stutter.

"Why not?"

"T ... too tired," was Baby's thin little reply.

He was crouching low, hiding his face from the fearsome dinosaurs.

"But ... don't you think your family might be worried about you?" said Clarasaurus.

The other dinosaurs nodded, pleased that Clarasaurus was handling this. They had no idea what you were supposed to do with a baby dragon stuck on your mountain. They only really knew about things like charging and chanting and being fierce.

Chapter 6

On the Flames-are-us Mountain there was chaos. The dragons were rushing about all over the place, getting even slimier than usual in the rain and banging into each other in the darkness.

"Baby! Where are you!" they cried out.

But of course there was no reply.

"He must have got left behind!" said Mumma Dragon, her voice filled with panic. "I'm flying over there to find him."

"Don't be silly, Mumma!" said Grandpa. "Those dinosaurs would have you for supper!"

"They might have poor Baby if I don't get there first and stop them," Mumma replied.

"Calm down," said Daddio. "We need to think of a plan. Let's get back in the dry."

So everyone followed Daddio towards the cavern. Everyone except Mumma Dragon, that is. Mumma slipped away, spread her wings and took off silently into the dismal night air. She was very afraid of facing the dinosaurs on her own. But what else could she do?

On Scarytops Mountain Clarasaurus had just made a decision. "Poor little baby thing can't fly so I'm going to take him back home," she announced.

"What!" bellowed Sebasaurus.

"Don't be ridiculous!" said Lucasaurus.

"Those dragons would have you for supper!" added Christophersaurus.

"But what is to be done with the little one then?" asked Clara. "Look at him, scared out of his wits. He wants his mumma!"

Clarasaurus had spoken so gently that Baby Dragon dared to raise his eyes and see what the face of a dinosaur looked like. He got a surprise because he was expecting something gruesome and terrible but Clarasaurus actually looked very kindly.

"Let's have a proper meeting to discuss what is to be done," said Sebasaurus. "We'll go to the campus."

"Good idea," agreed the other dinosaurs. And they all went lolloping after him.

All but Clarasaurus, that is. Clarasaurus picked up Baby Dragon gently and whispered, "Don't worry, little fellow. I'll take you back to your mumma." Then, when no one was looking, she padded off down the mountainside.

Chapter 7

Mumma Dragon had a big surprise as she flew over the valley. One of the dinosaurs was walking down the hill opposite. She seemed to be carrying something. Mumma peered down into the darkness.

"Hey that's my mumma!" Baby Dragon told Clarasaurus. "See! Up there!"

"I don't think she's spotted us," said Clara, her heart racing with fear. The mumma dragon was sure to be cross. "Coo-ee! Down here!" she called in a shaky voice.

Mumma Dragon couldn't believe her eyes or her ears. She flew down and alighted in the valley. "Baby! Baby!" she cried. "Are you all right? Has the nasty dinosaur hurt you?"

"No," Baby answered in a strong voice. "This is Clarasaurus. She's been looking after me."

Clarasaurus took Baby right up to where Mumma was waiting in the valley. She set him gently on the ground. "There you are."

Mumma Dragon and Clarasaurus Dinosaur stared at each other. Baby Dragon looked from one to the other. "Thank you," said Mumma eventually. "I was afraid … afraid …" Mumma trailed off because she wasn't really sure what she was afraid of.

"We'd never hurt a baby," said Clarasaurus firmly. Then she looked down, and when she looked back up she seemed rather embarrassed. "Well, the truth is, we'd never hurt anyone. Not even a fly. It's just a bit of fun. Dinosaurs like roaring and charging, that's all."

"Same with us," said Mumma, her eyes twinkling. "We dragons like to swoop around and puff out fire! It's silly really." Then Clara and Mumma looked at each other again and suddenly burst out laughing. They laughed and they laughed till the mountains shook.

"Are we friends with the dinosaurs now?" asked Baby.

"Yes, I think we are," said Mumma.

"Good," Baby said. "My plan worked!"

Then Mumma and Clara looked at Baby, their mouths hanging open in amazement.

"You mean you got left behind on purpose?" asked Clarasaurus.

"Yep," said Baby.

"Then you're one smart dragon!" smiled Clara, patting his head.

"Such a clever little thing!" said Mumma, hugging Baby. Then she turned to Clarasaurus. "Pop back and get the others. You're all invited to a party at our place!"

So that's exactly what Clarasaurus did. And a little later when the rain had stopped, the moon came out and shone down on the dancing dragons and dinosaurs. Never had the mountains seen such a party as this. In fact you could say it was a roaring success!

Chapter 1

A dinosaur popped her head over the top of a mountain. Her name was Gemmasaurus. She narrowed her eyes and stared hard. Was that a little smoke curl she just spotted rising up from the Flames-are-us Mountain opposite? Or did her eyes deceive her?

Alexandersaurus came padding up behind her on his gigantic flat feet.

"Aargh!" screamed Gemmasaurus. "Don't do that Alexander. You made me a jump!"

"Sorry," said Alexandersaurus, in his gravelly whisper. "I can't help being a quiet guy. Anyway, can you see anything?" he added.

"I think I spied smoke!" replied Gemmasaurus.

Alexander craned his long neck. "Smoke means dragons! Hurray! Are we going to scare them?"

"Hang on," Gemma replied. "We've got to wait till I'm quite sure."

On the Flames-are-us Mountain sat a large family of dragons conducting an important meeting.

Every time one of them spoke, a little bit of fire swished into the cold air then disappeared in a flash. Occasionally it left a curl of smoke which rose and rose, growing wispier and wispier.

"What are we going to do about those wicked dinosaurs on Scarytops Mountain?" asked Grandpa Dragon. "I'm fed up with the way they keep charging over here trying to frighten us."

"Me too," said Grandma Dragon. "I'm too old to have to keep watch. I get tired."

Baby Dragon cocked his head. When he spoke, a glittering sparkler came out of his mouth because he was too little to have proper flames. "I don't understand," he squeaked. "Why do we have to keep watch?"

Daddio Dragon reared up on his hind legs. "Haven't you learnt anything, Baby?
We keep watch so that when the dinosaurs come to attack us we can fly up in the air!"

"Yes and scare them back with our fire and our shrieks!" added Bigboy Dragon, grinning his head off.

"Why?" asked Baby simply.

"Because!" said Bigboy.

"Oh," said Baby, wearing a puzzled frown.

Block Your Ears!
Here It Comes!

CD tracks 1 and 2

1. Creep - ing   a - long   with   a   di - no - saur____

Creep - ing   a - long   with   a   di - no - saur____

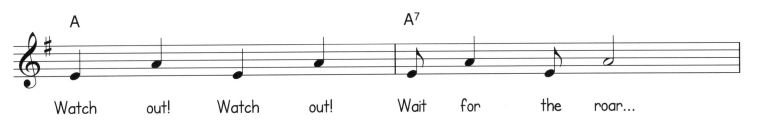

Watch   out!   Watch   out!   Wait   for   the   roar...

Block   your   ears!   Here   it   comes!   ROAR!

2. Marching along with a dinosaur...

3. Striding along with a dinosaur...

4. Skipping along with a dinosaur...

5. Jumping along with a dinosaur...

Let's Sing!
(CD tracks 1 and 2)

⬇ This is great fun but it's hard to sing and do the stepping at the same time, so have half the class singing and half doing the actions. You can either swap for each verse or swap at the end of the whole song. Keep doing the relevant action during the third line of each verse, then stand still and block your ears for the last line. The children might like to join in with the roar on the CD.

⬇ Another way to perform the song is to place a few hand drums on the floor in the middle of the room, then all creep/march/stride/skip/jump around in a wide circle until the words 'Watch out!' which are the cue for everyone to stand still. At this point, a few pre-allocated children go to the middle and beat the drums for the 'roar'. Choose different children to play the drums for each verse.

Sorting dinosaurs
This is a good opportunity for two sorting activities.

1) Sort dinosaurs into meet eaters and plant eaters.

2) Sort them into dinosaurs on land, sky and water.

Dinosaurus names

In this chapter we meet Gemmasaurus and Alexandersaurus. But can the children remember any other of the dinosaurs' names?

Why have the dinosaurs got these funny names? Talk about names of types of real dinosaurs such as Tyrannosaurus Rex and Brontosaurus, Triceratops and Iguanodon. Look at pictures of all the various types. (In Chapter 3 we look at the comparative body shapes in more detail.)

Try adapting the names of the children in your class into dinosaur language. Can they work them out for themselves?

Dinosaur names on the drum

🐾 The children sit in a circle and each has a turn of tapping the syllables of their dinosaur name. Practise counting the sounds of the name and making sure you match that with the right number of taps on the drum.

🐾 Group the children so all those with three sounds sit together, e.g. Pipsaurus, those with four sounds sit together, e.g. Alfiesaurus, those with five sit together, e.g. Natashasaurus and those with six, e.g. Arabellasaurus.

🐾 Now you play a series of taps on the drum. If you play three, the children with three sounds in the names must stand up etc.

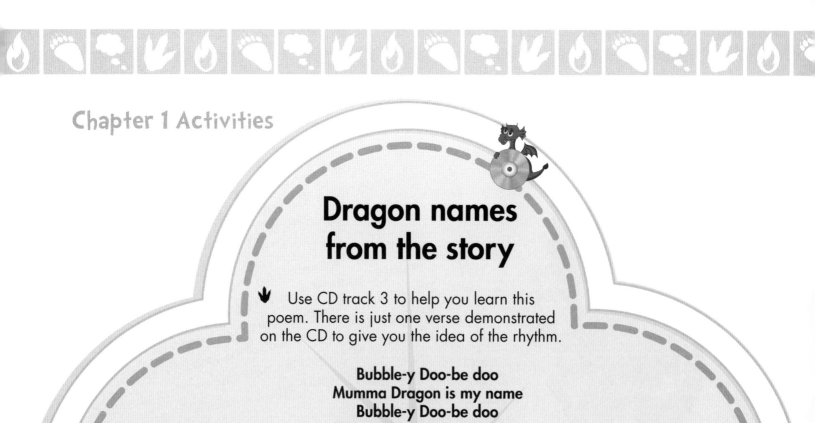

Dragon names from the story

🐾 Use CD track 3 to help you learn this poem. There is just one verse demonstrated on the CD to give you the idea of the rhythm.

Bubble-y Doo-be doo
Mumma Dragon is my name
Bubble-y Doo-be doo
Mumma Dragon is my name
Bubble-y Doo-be doo
Mumma Dragon is my name
I'm Mumma Dragon,
Bubble-y Doo.
Who are you?

Bubble-y Doo-be doo
Daddio dragon is my name…

🐾 Continue like this with Grandpa Dragon, Grandma Dragon, Baby Dragon etc.

🐾 Can the children remember the whole family of dragons?

🐾 This is a great opportunity to talk about the families of the children in your class, their different sizes and components. Use mathematical language – small, medium, large.

🐾 Now try the poem using the children's own names. They should stand in a circle and say the poem with you as you walk round the outside of the circle. You stop on the words 'Who are you?' and lightly tap the child you are standing next to at that point on the head, or just look at them. Use the name of that child for the following verse. If they can manage to say e.g. 'Euan Dragon is my name' and 'I'm Euan Dragon' or 'Sunisa Dragon is my name' and 'I'm Sunisa Dragon' each time on their own, that's great, otherwise all say it together.

That made me a jump!

↓ Remember how Alexandersaurus made Gemmasaurus jump by creeping right up to her?

↓ You tap a drum very lightly whilst all the children creep around on tiptoe in time to your beat. They should keep an eye on you and when you do a big bang, they should all jump in the air.

↓ Now reverse the idea. All the children have instruments which they should tap very gently in time to the beat of your feet tiptoeing along. When you suddenly jump, they must each play one loud sound. This is hard to get perfectly in unison, but that is the objective!

Dinosaur family
Talk about whether the dinosaurs in the story are all different members of a big family like the dragons or whether they're just friends. If they are a family, which one might be the daddy, the mummy etc.

Your magical classroom
Make a large dinosaur/dragon egg and hide it in the classroom. Let the children find it and talk about what might hatch out.

What other animals hatch out of eggs?

Let the children draw/paint/sculpt what they think might hatch out of the egg.

Numeracy
How many dragons have been mentioned so far in the story?

How many dinosaurs' names can the children remember?

Give each child the name of one of the dragons or one of the dinosaurs. Let the remaining children, if there are any, or you yourself count how many that makes altogether.

Chapter 2

On Scarytops Mountain the dinosaurs were preparing for battle. How they beamed. They loved charging into the valley and up the Flames-are-us Mountain opposite.

"Show us your claws, Luca!" some of the young dinosaurs cried. "Let's see if they've grown!"

Lucasaurus smiled round proudly. "Yes, they're over half a metre long now. Bigger than a garden rake!"

The young dinosaurs turned to Annasaurus. "Give us a growl, Anna!"

Then everyone shivered and clung to each other because when Annasaurus growled the whole mountain shook.

"Those dragons are going to be terrified!" giggled Gemmasauras.

"Yes, but don't growl until we've got right up to them!" Christophersaurus said in a bit of a bossy voice. "You're always giving the game away, Anna!"

"Sorry," said Annasaurus. I just can't help myself!"

"OK, time for the pre-battle chant," announced Sebasaurus. "Gather round on the campus, everyone!"

There was a great deal of shuffling into position and when all the dinosaurs had formed a neat circle, Seb stood tall in the middle, his long neck stretched upward, his head flung back to the dark sky, and cried, "Let the chanting begin! One two THREE...!"

We're off to scare the dragons
We're off to scare the dragons
We're off to scare the dragons into the air
To give them a *fright!*

We're off to scare the dragons
We're off to scare the dragons
We're off to scare the dragons into the air
To *night!*

We're off to scare the dragons
We're off to scare the dragons
We're off to scare the dragons into the air
That's right!

Dinosaurus Action!

CD tracks 4 and 5

1. In our four-us, in our four-us, Do-ing the di - no - suar - us roar - us

In our four-us, in our four-us, Do-ing the di - no - suar - us roar - us

Roar!   Roar!   Roar!   Roar!

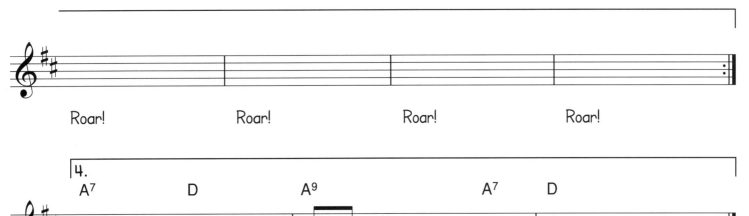

- saur - us   chor - us...   Di - nos   rule   O   K!

2. In our four-us, in our four-us
   Doing the dinosaurus floor-us...
   (all stomp on the four beats)

3. In our four-us, in our four-us
   Doing the dinosaurus claw-rus...
   (take turns stretching out 'claws' on the four beats)

4. In our four-us, in our four-us
   Doing the dinosaurus chorus...
   Dinos rule OK!

Let's Sing!
(CD tracks 4 and 5)

This song has strong actions to accompany it with great opportunities for working precisely to the beat! When working with the backing track only, be aware of the rather long introduction and don't forget that there is music for the action at the end of each verse.

Let's listen!

Talk about what fossils are. Show pictures unless you have real examples for the children to see.

Listen to the 'Fossils' music on CD track 6. This is from *Carnival of the Animals* by Saint Saëns.

It is easiest to see the structure of the piece as follows: chorus, verse, chorus, verse, short chorus. First, simply stand still and count to eight four times during each of the first two choruses and twice during the final chorus. Listen to the music without counting between the choruses.

Still working with the music of the chorus only, try some accompanying actions instead of counting to eight. You might like to choose just two different actions, e.g. clapping and patting knees. Do eight claps then eight knee pats and repeat that to make up the chorus. At the end there will only be enough music to do the eight claps and the eight knee pats once each.

If you feel ambitious, try four different actions – one for each lot of eight beats. Here are some examples of what you might do: strum a pretend guitar, tap heads, shake fingers as though trying to shake them off your hands, open and close fingers from fists, push and pull something imaginary down and back up again, bend and straighten knees, tap toes. There are many possibilities. The children might be able to offer some ideas but avoid jumping unless you can do it neatly, as jumping is essentially two actions which might therefore 'spill out of' the beats.

Draw the children's attention to the extract of 'Twinkle Twinkle Little Star' embedded into the music between the first two choruses. Then notice that the music which follows the second chorus is much gentler than the previous 'listening' section, apart from one big flourish. Listen out for the flourish and when it comes, do an enormous circle with both arms and then you will be straight into your final chorus.

In this way you are creating a choreography.

Fossils with percussion

Now you are familiar with the music, try adding a musical accompaniment so the children are playing instruments along with the CD. Have four groups of children playing, e.g. tambourines, hand drums, shakers, claves. Take turns to play on the beat (eight beats each) for the chorus). You will have to 'conduct' and a big skill here is for the children to keep their eyes on you the whole time so they know when to start and when to stop.

Dinosaur chant

We're off to scare the dragons
We're off to scare the dragons
We're off to scare the dragons into the air
To give them a *fright!*

We're off to scare the dragons
We're off to scare the dragons
We're off to scare the dragons into the air
To-*night!*

We're off to scare the dragons
We're off to scare the dragons
We're off to scare the dragons into the air
That's *right!*

Have fun chanting this poem loudly. As you chant the first verse, clap in time with the beat. For the second verse, stamp in time with the beat and for the third, march round in time to the beat.

Chapter 3

"Who's on guard tonight?" asked Biggirl Dragon.

"Me," replied Auntie Dragon. "Worst luck," she added under her fiery breath.

"Don't fall asleep whatever you do!" said Uncle Dragon.

So whilst all the dragons found themselves cosy spots to snuggle into for a good night's sleep, Auntie Dragon sat right at the top of the Flames-are-us Mountain and looked up at the sky. There was only one star shining and she started to imagine what its name might be. "I know," she said to herself, "I'll try to think of star names beginning with every letter of the alphabet. That will keep me awake." So she did. But she'd only got as far as G for Gorgonzola when her eyelids started to droop, then her head began to loll, and after a few seconds, from her half open mouth came a loud snoring that echoed right down the valley.

The dinosaurs had to stifle their giggles as they crept through the valley towards the Flames-are-us Mountain. They were only half way up, however, when the beautiful peace of the night was suddenly shattered by the most almighty roar.

"Sorry everyone!" wailed Annasaurus a second later. "I couldn't help it. It just slipped out!"

"You silly creature!" shouted Christophersaurus as there came a different kind of roar from the Flames-are-us Mountain — the roar of fire erupting from the nostrils of the dragons. And next minute there was a violent beating and flapping of wings as the whole family rose into the air.

"Well done, Auntie!" cried Daddio Dragon enthusiastically. "I never knew you could roar such a loud warning!" Then he flew down towards the dinosaurs calling, "You'll never catch us. We're cleverer by far than you!"

The dinosaurs thought they would look rather foolish if they admitted it had been one of them who had roared, so they just leapt off in enormous bounds, growling, "We'll get you one of these days! You just wait!"

But little Ellenasaurus was falling behind because of her unusually short legs and in the end Clarasaurus had to scoop her up and run along carrying her.

All in all it was a big relief to get home.

Twinkling Stars

CHORUS

The sky is black, the sky is black, It's ve - ry dark up there.___ Then

just when you think there's not a sin - gle star, You blink and then you stare at...

1. One twink - ling star, one twink - ling star, One twink - ling star in the night.

One twink - ling star, one twink - ling star, Oh what a pret - ty sight!___

2. Two twinkling stars, two twinkling stars,
   Two twinkling stars in the night.
   Two twinkling stars, two twinkling stars,
   Oh what a pretty sight!

3. Three twinkling stars, three twinkling stars,
   Three twinkling stars in the night.
   Three twinkling stars, three twinkling stars,
   Oh what a pretty sight!

   (Continue with four or more pretty stars!)

Let's Sing!
(CD tracks 7 and 8)

❧ This is a very gentle yet powerful song that children love to sing.

❧ Place a pair of finger chimes (or a triangle) somewhere in the hall with space around it. Then in another spot in the hall place two finger chimes, and in a third spot, place three.

❧ In the first verse, one chosen child plays the finger chimes to represent the one twinkling star whilst the other children all dance round him/her. Similarly for the second and third verses.

❧ All the children simply stand still in a space of their own and sing during the choruses.

Relax!

❧ Track 8 is a lovely long peaceful track which you might simply like to play as calming background music.

Four beats and three beats take turns

❧ Sing 'Twinkle Twinkle Little Star'.

❧ Now divide the class into two groups. Sing the song again but this time accompany with claps. This is an exercise in being alert because the children are taking turns but each turn is very short. So the first group do four claps to the exact beats of the words Twin-kle twin-kle then switch quickly to the next group who do three claps to the exact beat of the words lit-tle star. Continue like this. You will find the four/three pattern will work throughout the song.

Stars coming out!

🌱 Every child has an instrument that makes a gentle star-like sound. You might have to improvise with spoons and cups if you don't have enough finger cymbals, triangles and little bells. The children should be dotted around the room, standing up.

🌱 The children must look at you all the time, so this task takes focus! When you point to a child, they make their star come out by playing one sound on their instrument and then quickly sitting down. Pick the children in random order then when they are all sitting down, start pointing once again to indicate they should play then stand up.

Dinosaur shapes and sizes

You have already compared different pictures of dinosaurs and talked about their different names.

Now look carefully at their different body proportions. Isolate the various body parts to make comparisons. Discuss how their different-shaped limbs, wings, bodies, heads, feet, claws might affect their living.

We know that Elenasaurus has short legs. Talk about how the other dinosaurs might look.

Draw and colour pictures of them.

Slow beats, fast beats

🌱 You beat a drum very slowly, using a big action. The children must clap in time to this very slow beat. They should let their hands span out wide to fill up the time needed between beats. Now play at a medium speed so the clap is not so wide. Then try a fast beat so the children must keep their hands very close together or they won't be able to keep up with the beat. Small children find it very hard to clap fast. Encouraging the tiniest movement is the best way forward!

Short legs, long legs

🌱 Like Ellenasaurus, take short steps around while you play a beat on a drum. When you change to a slow beat the children must stride out. Did they notice that you played more slowly for the long legged stride?

Dancing smoke and flames

Try dancing freely with the music on CD track 9. Stay in your own spot at first but face different directions and move at different levels (low, medium, high) as you roll your hands over and over, stretch and sway, twist and turn freely representing the smoke and/or flames. When you hear the change in the music, you can continue your movement around the room. When children are free to move around a room, they tend to just run. Draw their attention to the fact that they are still dancing flames!

Fire art

Talk about the colours of flames. How many subtle shades of yellow, orange and red can you make by mixing paints? Paint the various colours of flames on a black background.

'Flames' Poem

Talk about the movement you've just done. How did the children feel? What words can you find to describe the movements: swishing, leaping, stretching, twirling, curling, turning, zipping, darting, diving, zooming, whizzing, flickering, swaying etc.

Can you make a class poem about the flames?

Words and movement – the grand performance

For a grand performance, some children move to the music while some children say the poem at the same time.

Short sounds, long sounds

❧ Take a drum and a pair of finger chimes or any instrument that rings. Play one beat on the drum. Point out to the children that the beat made a short sound and then stopped. Now play the chimes and let the children hear how long the chime rings on.

❧ Now all the children are going to count to four repeatedly with a steady even beat whilst you play your drum on the first beat only of each lot of four. The children must check you are doing this correctly. Notice that when you are all chanting the words 'two', 'three', 'four' there is no sound from the drum.

❧ Try the same thing with the bell. Did the children notice that the bell rang on throughout the four beats each time?

❧ Can the children say which other instruments ring on and which only have a short sound?

❧ Divide the class into two. Give half the children instruments which can produce sounds which ring on, and give the other half instruments which can only make short sounds. Take turns to play a sound counting repeatedly to four, so the group with short sounds play on count number 1 and stay silent for counts 2, 3 and 4, then the other group play on beat 1 and count the other three beats, noticing the sound ringing on. Continue to take turns like this.

Slowly and quickly up and down

❧ Play your drum in exactly the same way and the children must bob down very quickly to a crouching position, on that first beat then stay down for beats two, three and four.

❧ Now play your bells in the same way. This time the children must take the whole four beats to go down to the crouching position and the whole four beats to slowly rise back up again.

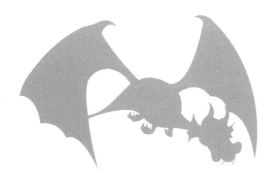

Chapter 4

"I'm not putting up with those dinosaur bullies for
another second!" declared Grandma Dragon.
"We need to teach them a lesson!"

"Quite agree!" nodded the others.

"Let's fly around their mountain singing songs and blowing out smoke to make
them cough and keep them awake all night!" suggested Littleboy Dragon.

"Can I just stay here?" asked Baby Dragon.

"Absolutely not!" Daddio replied. "You are quite old enough to join in."

So that night, the dragons waited until it was completely dark and then they silently rose into the air and swooped off
towards Scarytops Mountain. But when they were scarcely over the valley that separated the two mountains, there
came a sharp whip of lightning that lit up the sky, followed by a deep bass drum roll of thunder.

"Keep going!" commanded Daddio. "The rain won't start for a few minutes. We've still got time to scare the living
daylights out of them!"

"Don't be silly, Daddio!" said Mumma Dragon. "What's the point? You know our fire will be put out if it rains. Let's just
go home."

"We're almost there!" said Daddio. "Come on everyone. Why let a bit of rain put you off!" Then as he swooped over
Scarytops Mountain, he opened his mouth and let out a great ball of bright amber fire.

At that very moment the clouds above crashed against each other, and down came lashing needles of rain.
Daddio tried to let out another burst of fire but it was no good. The moment the rain hit his flames, they fizzled
into nothingness.

"Ha ha!" laughed the dinosaurs, looking up at the soaking wet dragons.
"You've lost your fire! Serves you right!"

"Come on!" cried Uncle Dragon. "Let's get back.
We're getting soaked. Hurry! Hurry!"

"Shelter in caves!" called Grandpa Dragon, flying very high so that his
enormous wings would protect the smaller dragons from the rain.

And all this time not one single one of the dragons had noticed that someone
was missing. Poor little Baby Dragon had been left behind because he didn't
have any flap left in his wings, nor any squeak in his voice to call out. So he
just lay down on Scarytops Mountain in the middle of all the Dinosaurs.

The Rain Came Down And Down

CD tracks 10 and 11

Am ... **F**

1. First there was the light - ning   ve - ry   ve - ry   fright -'ning

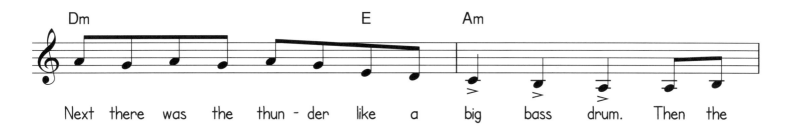

Dm ... **E** ... **Am**

Next there was the thun - der like a   big   bass   drum.   Then the

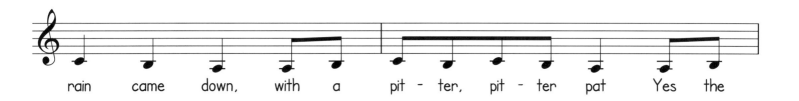

rain   came   down,   with   a   pit - ter,   pit - ter   pat   Yes   the

E⁷ ... **A**

rain   came   down   and   down.

2. First there was the lightning
   Very, very fright'ning
   Next there was the thunder like a big bass drum.
   Then the rain came down with a drip, drip, drop
   Yes the rain came down and down.

3. First there was the lightning
   Very, very fright'ning
   Next there was the thunder like a big bass drum.
   Then the rain came down with a splash, splash, splosh
   Yes the rain came down and down.

Making shakers

Use smallish containers made of tin, plastic or Tupperware. Fill them with dried rice or pulses, 'hundreds and thousands' or anything else you can think of.

Make sure the children see what goes inside the various shakers and make the connection with the sound that is then produced. A lighter filling will produce a lighter sound, a denser one, a heavier sound.

Let's Sing!
(CD tracks 10 and 11)

⬇ Use CD track 10 to help you learn the song and simply enjoy singing with a bit of action for the rain with the usual descending finger action.

Singing songs to keep the dinosaurs awake

⬇ Littleboy dragon suggests singing songs and blowing out smoke to keep the dinosaurs awake all night. Which songs would be the best for keeping the dinosaurs awake – loud ones or quiet ones?

⬇ Have fun singing your favourites.

Accompany the song with percussion

⬇ Use the shakers to play on the rain part of each verse of the song. Let the children decide which shakers would be best to accompany 'pitter patter' 'drip, drip' and 'splash, splash', each accompaniment slightly louder than the previous one.

⬇ Next ask the children to suggest a sound to accompany the lightning and then the thunder. In the absence of a 'big bass drum'(!), a cymbal hit with a beater makes a satisfying thunder sound as it rings on. If you use a small drum, you might find the sound a little 'dry'! Warn the children that the cymbal sound will be loud. Start by beating it gently, then gradually louder as they get used to the sound. Remember to hold the cymbal up and away from your body so the sound can ring.

Spreading fire

Talk about how fire spreads.

🐾 The children sit in a semi-circle, each child with an instrument. The first child plays his instrument and then plays it close to the second child's instrument. The second child then joins in playing, as though his instrument has 'caught' the sound, just as a fire would spread. Continue along the semi-circle like this, the sound getting louder and louder as more and more children join in.

🐾 Mime the action of throwing a bucket of water over the children as a signal to stop! Did everyone stop at exactly the right moment?

I hear thunder

**I hear thunder, I hear thunder
Hush don't you, hush don't you.
Pitter patter raindrops,
pitter patter raindrops
I'm wet through. So are you!**

🐾 Sing the song to the tune of 'Frère Jacques'.

🐾 Now try chanting the words. Children find it difficult to chant words that they are used to singing. The reason for the chanting is that we are going to try this little rhyme in canon, or in a round. Small children cannot hold tunes when they are singing in canon but chanting is possible and effective.

🐾 You'll need one adult to accompany each of the two groups. Wait till the first group has chanted the first line, then the second group starts at the beginning of the song. Both groups are therefore chanting the whole rhyme at the same speed, keeping it nice and rhythmic, but one group always remains exactly one line ahead of the other group.

🐾 If you are very ambitious, you might like to try three or even four groups!

Chapter 5

The dragons couldn't wait to get out of the rain. They plunged into an enormous dark cavern where their eyes glinted and glimmered in the blackness.

"That was rubbish!" said Littleboy Dragon. "I hate the rain!"

"Me too!" Littlegirl Dragon agreed.

"Never mind that," said Daddio a bit grumpily. "We need to make a plan to pay those dinosaurs back. I can't stand it when they laugh at us!"

"As soon as this horrible rain stops we should fly back over there," suggested Bigboy Dragon. "They certainly won't be expecting us so soon."

"Baby Dragon will be too tired for that," pointed out Mumma Dragon. Then she suddenly stood on her hind legs and whipped her head from side to side, trying to see in the dim light of the cave. "Where are you, Baby Dragon?" she called, her voice echoing round the cavern.

For a few moments a wondering silence fell over the dragons and nothing could be seen but darting, flicking eyes. Then Bigboy Dragon spoke. "Don't worry about Baby. He's always wandering off. He'll be somewhere around."

"I'm going to look for him," said Mumma Dragon. And off she went.

Meanwhile Clarasaurus was bending over Baby Dragon. She wasn't sure what to say. But someone had to say something. The other dinosaurs were just staring at Baby as though he was an alien.

"... hadn't you better go and find your family?" mumbled Clarasaurus eventually.

"I ... I can't," Baby Dragon said in a stutter.

"Why not?"

"T ... too tired," was Baby's thin little reply.

He was crouching low, hiding his face from the fearsome dinosaurs.

"But ... don't you think your family might be worried about you?" said Clarasaurus.

The other dinosaurs nodded, pleased that Clarasaurus was handling this. They had no idea what you were supposed to do with a baby dragon stuck on your mountain. They only really knew about things like charging and chanting and being fierce.

Hush Little Baby

CD tracks 12 and 13

1. Hush lit-tle ba - by   no need to cry   Ma-ma's gon-na sing you a   lul - la - by.

If that lul - la - by's no fun   Ma-ma's gon-na get you the shi - ny sun.

If that shiny sun goes in

Mama's gonna give you a great big grin,

If that grin is no surprise

Mama's gonna get you the wide blue skies,

If those skies don't make you smile

Mama's gonna get you a golden mile,

If that mile's too far to go

Mama's gonna get you a bright red bow,

If that bright red bow's too big

Mama's gonna get you a guinea pig,

If that guinea pig won't talk

Mama's gonna take you on a magic walk

Up to the moon and down to your bed

Hush little baby sleepy head.

Let's Sing!

(CD tracks 12 and 13)

🐾 Baby dragon is the focus of this chapter, so here is a lullaby for a baby.

Can you see Baby?

🐾 Learn the poem with the help of the CD track 14, adding appropriate actions.

🐾 Divide the class into groups of three. Each little group takes turns to say the poem. Play the backing track (15) as many times as necessary.

Eyes are flicking (flick flick)
Heads are whipping (whip whip)
Bodies twitching (twitch twitch)
Can you see Baby? No. No. No!

🐾 Now try with percussion, without the CD, but try to keep the beat steady. Number the children 1, 2 and 3 in each group. Either work with all the groups at once or one group at a time. Say the words all together.

🐾 Eyes are flicking (Number 1s play two beats on an instrument, e.g. woodbocks on the two flicks)
Heads are whipping (Number 2s play a different instrument on the two whips)
Bodies twitching (Number 3s play a different instrument again on the two twitches)
Can you see Baby? No. No. No! (All play three quick beats on 'No. No. No!')

Eyes in the dark composition

🌱 You are going to improvise a piece of music using as many homemade sounds as possible for the background darkness.

🌱 Tell the class you are going to make a piece of music together which is all about the dark cavern and the bright glittering eyes gleaming and flickering in the darkness. Talk about how magical that is, and how the darkness is the background but it's not just nothingness. Try to convey that the darkness is a positive presence. Sometimes it is completely dark; at other times there might be only one or two flickers; at other times there might be more.

🌱 Half the children are going to be representing the darkness of the cavern, and the other half, the dragons' eyes glinting and gleaming.

🌱 If you gently rub your nails round and round a surface, it will make a sound that you might like to use. See how many sounds you can find in the classroom and then decide which ones would be the best to use. Some might sound too metallic or harsh or just too quiet to be heard. These children are representing the darkness.

🌱 The other children, representing the flickering stars, should have bells or triangles or even a xylophone or glock. You can have two children to a glock and it doesn't matter which notes they play.

🌱 The children must exercise great self-control and without being directed by you, only play very occasionally. Try to look at each other and not to be 'greedy' with the allowance of 'eye flickers' – just two or three each.

🌱 With a finger to your lips, make a big deal of being absolutely silent before you start the piece. When you are ready for the background darkness music to start, give a little nod to those children. They must be watching you carefully. Decide who will play the first of the 'flickering eye' sounds but thereafter it's up to the children to organise their sounds sparingly. After about a minute, raise your hand for the flickerings to stop and allow the background darkness to continue for another few seconds, then put a hand up to stop the whole piece, and a finger to your lips for silence.

🌱 Swap parts.

Perform, record, listen, improve, repeat

When you think the 'Eyes In The Dark' composition from the previous page sounds ready to perform (i.e. the flickerings are sparing enough!), record it. Explain to the children that for this they need to be totally silent before you start and totally silent at the end. Remind them about your hand signals.

Listen back to the piece with eyes closed and try to imagine you are a dragon in the cavern.

Dragon art
Make pictures of the eyes in the darkness. Paint a dark wash for the background and then add glitter or shiny sticky paper in tiny eye shapes for the eyes.

Numeracy
This is a good opportunity to focus on even numbers - one pair, two pairs, three, four, five pairs of eyes.

Odd
one out

⬇ This activity is reflective
of the fact that Mumma Dragon
thought and acted differently from the
other dragons. Talk about the decision
she made and the reason she might have
made it. Also, Clarasaurus acted differently
from the other dinosaurs. Talk about in what
way she was different and why
that might have been.

⬇ For the activity, one child, either blindfolded or with
eyes closed and hands over eyes, sits in the middle of a circle
of children. Give one of the children in the circle an instrument
such as a tambourine. That child (the odd man out) jangles the
tambourine. Can the child in the middle point to where the sound is
coming from without looking.

⬇ Make this activity harder by letting all the other children in the circle clap at
the same time as the child plays the instrument. Can the blindfolded
child point to where the sound of the instrument is
coming from, despite the off-putting claps?

Stranger danger
This is a good opportunity
to talk about what to do
when you are lost and lead
to 'stranger danger'. Maybe
invite a local PC to visit and
talk in assembly.

Chapter 6

On the Flames-are-us Mountain there was chaos. The dragons were rushing about all over the place, getting even slimier than usual in the rain and banging into each other in the darkness.

"Baby! Where are you!" they cried out.

But of course there was no reply.

"He must have got left behind!" said Mumma Dragon, her voice filled with panic.
"I'm flying over there to find him."

"Don't be silly, Mumma!" said Grandpa. "Those dinosaurs would have you for supper!"

"They might have poor Baby if I don't get there first and stop them," Mumma replied.

"Calm down," said Daddio. "We need to think of a plan. Let's get back in the dry."

So everyone followed Daddio towards the cavern. Everyone except Mumma Dragon, that is. Mumma slipped away, spread her wings and took off silently into the dismal night air. She was very afraid of facing the dinosaurs on her own. But what else could she do?

On Scarytops Mountain Clarasaurus had just made a decision. "Poor little baby thing can't fly so I'm going to take him back home," she announced.

"What!" bellowed Sebasaurus.

"Don't be ridiculous!" said Lucasaurus.

"Those dragons would have you for supper!" added Christophersaurus.

"But what is to be done with the little one then?" asked Clara. "Look at him, scared out of his wits. He wants his mumma!"

Clarasaurus had spoken so gently that Baby Dragon dared to raise his eyes and see what the face of a dinosaur looked like. He got a surprise because he was expecting something gruesome and terrible but Clarasaurus actually looked very kindly.

"Let's have a proper meeting to discuss what is to be done," said Sebasaurus. "We'll go to the campus."

"Good idea," agreed the other dinosaurs. And they all went lolloping after him.

All but Clarasaurus, that is. Clarasaurus picked up Baby Dragon gently and whispered, "Don't worry, little fellow. I'll take you back to your mumma." Then, when no one was looking, she padded off down the mountainside.

Rock A Bye Baby

CD tracks 16 and 17

1. Safe in his cave the ba - by bear lies,

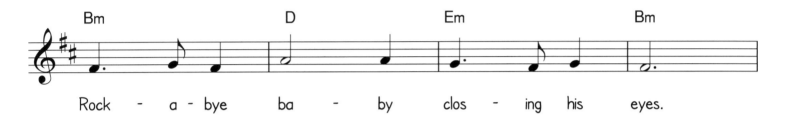

Rock - a - bye ba - by clos - ing his eyes.

Mum - my bear checks her ba - by's a - sleep.

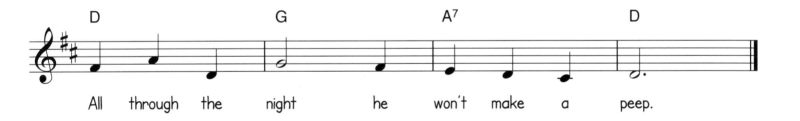

All through the night he won't make a peep.

2. Safe in the jungle baby snake lies,
   Rock-a-bye baby closing his eyes,
   Mummy snake checks her baby's asleep,
   All through the night he won't make a peep.

3. Safe in the woods the baby mouse lies...

4. Safe on the farm the baby pig lies...

5. Safe in the pond the baby duck lies...

Let's Sing!
(CD tracks 16 and 17)

🦶 Baby dragon remains the focus in this chapter and now we see how protective both Mumma Dragon and Clarasaurus feel towards him. Talk about that. Learn the song with track 16. You will hear mention of many different animals and their mothers.

🦶 The song is a gentle lullaby so use gentle voices to sing. You might like to sway with very small sways from side to side as you sing.

🦶 Can you invent new verses maybe about the sea, the zoo, the hills?

Three-time

🦶 This song is in three-time. This means you can count three equal beats repeatedly throughout the song, and the first one is the most important of the three.

🦶 Listen to the backing track on the CD (17) and whisper 'one, two, three' repeatedly in time with the music.

🦶 Now try just saying the 'one' each time and saying 'two' and 'three' inside your head.

🦶 Next try patting knees on one and doing two gentle claps on two and three. Young children find this coordination difficult but very satisfying when they've achieved it!

Listen to a lullaby

🦶 Listen to the famous Brahms 'Lullaby' on the CD track 18. This piece is also in three-time but it is at a much slower tempo than the song.

Song time

🦶 Listen to the following well-known songs on the CD (tracks 19–24).

🦶 Join in with each one then try to work out if it is in three-time or four-time.

Sing A Song Of Sixpence (4)
Mary Mary Quite Contrary (4)
Where Oh Where Has My Little Dog Gone? (3)
Away In A Manger (3)
Lavender's Blue (3)
Twinkle Twinkle Little Star (4)

Marching music

🌱 The opposite of a lullaby might be marching music. Sing 'The Grand Old Duke Of York'. Start with a salute then march around for the first four lines. Stand still for the next four lines and point up, then down on the relevant words, and show 'half way' with a flat hand. Finish with two claps and a salute.

Oh the grand old duke of York
He had ten thousand men
He marched them up to the top of the hill
And he marched then down again.

And when they were up they were up,
And when they were down they were down.
And when they were only half way up
They were neither up nor down.

🌱 Ask a few strong singers who know the song well to sing it whilst the others whisper 'one, two, one, two' etc repeatedly in time with the singing. So, this song is in two-time.

Three-time and four-time accompaniments

🐾 Play each rhyme/song again and notice the beats on the CD that accompany each one. Can you hear that the first of the three or of the four beats is slightly louder than the others?

🐾 Play the songs again and clap on these strong beats only.

🐾 Now try gently playing a percussion instrument on the slightly louder beat each time. Only have a few children for each song/rhyme so you don't drown out the music. The others should be listening to see who is accompanying well.

Chapter 7

Mumma Dragon had a big surprise as she flew over the valley. One of the dinosaurs was walking down the hill opposite. She seemed to be carrying something. Mumma peered down into the darkness.

"Hey that's my mumma!" Baby Dragon told Clarasaurus. "See! Up there!"

"I don't think she's spotted us," said Clara, her heart racing with fear. The mumma dragon was sure to be cross. "Coo-ee! Down here!" she called in a shaky voice.

Mumma Dragon couldn't believe her eyes or her ears. She flew down and alighted in the valley. "Baby! Baby!" she cried. "Are you all right? Has the nasty dinosaur hurt you?"

"No," Baby answered in a strong voice. "This is Clarasaurus. She's been looking after me."

Clarasaurus took Baby right up to where Mumma was waiting in the valley. She set him gently on the ground. "There you are."

Mumma Dragon and Clarasaurus Dinosaur stared at each other. Baby Dragon looked from one to the other. "Thank you," said Mumma eventually. "I was afraid ... afraid ..." Mumma trailed off because she wasn't really sure what she was afraid of.

"We'd never hurt a baby," said Clarasaurus firmly. Then she looked down, and when she looked back up she seemed rather embarrassed. "Well, the truth is, we'd never hurt anyone. Not even a fly. It's just a bit of fun. Dinosaurs like roaring and charging, that's all."

"Same with us," said Mumma, her eyes twinkling. "We dragons like to swoop around and puff out fire! It's silly really." Then Clara and Mumma looked at each other again and suddenly burst out laughing. They laughed and they laughed till the mountains shook.

"Are we friends with the dinosaurs now?" asked Baby.

"Yes, I think we are," said Mumma.

"Good," Baby said. "My plan worked!"

Then Mumma and Clara looked at Baby, their mouths hanging open in amazement.

"You mean you got left behind on purpose?" asked Clarasaurus.

"Yep," said Baby.

"Then you're one smart dragon!" smiled Clara, patting his head.

"Such a clever little thing!" said Mumma, hugging Baby. Then she turned to Clarasaurus. "Pop back and get the others. You're all invited to a party at our place!"

So that's exactly what Clarasaurus did. And a little later when the rain had stopped, the moon came out and shone down on the dancing dragons and dinosaurs. Never had the mountains seen such a party as this. In fact you could say it was a roaring success!

Let's Have A Party

CD tracks 25 and 26

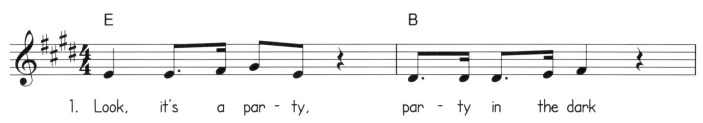

1. Look, it's a par - ty, par - ty in the dark

Look, it's a par - ty, par - ty in the dark, Well there are

dra - gons____ and di - no - saurs____ Oh

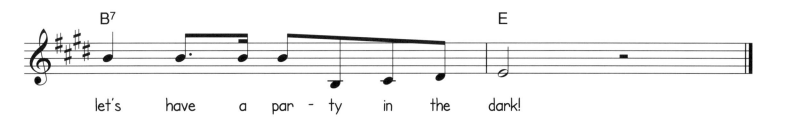

let's have a par - ty in the dark!

2. Look they are dancing, dancing in the dark
   Look they are dancing, dancing in the dark,
   Well there are dragons and dinosaurs
   Oh let's have a party in the dark!

3. Look they are swaying, swaying in the dark...

4. Look they are flying, flying in the dark...

5. Look they are playing, playing in the dark...

Chapter 7 Activities

Let's Sing!
(CD tracks 25 and 26)

🌱 Place enough instruments around the outside of the room for each child to have one. The children should sit in a space to sing the first verse then stand and do the actions as indicated in each subsequent verse. For the last verse, they should pick up the instrument nearest to them and play it in time to the beat.

Party games

🌱 This is a great opportunity for playing a whole range of party games including the usual Musical Bumps, Musical Statues, Musical Chairs and Musical Mats, all of which are good for listening and quick reactions. Remember, for Musical Statues and Bumps, rather than just dancing, you can do set actions to the music you are listening to, e.g. touching heads for four beats then bending knees for four beats etc. This means you have to concentrate on doing the actions whilst at the same time listening for the music to stop.

Pass the percussion

🌱 This is like Pass the Parcel but you pass a tambourine round the circle, each child doing two taps and a shake then passing the tambourine on to the next child. The musical skill here is to keep within the rhythmic framework. There is a backing track on the CD (track 27) to get you started, with a little rhyme to show you how to fit the taps, shakes and passing on into the music. You will find there are all sorts of pop songs and pieces of instrumental music which will provide a suitable backing track for the beat you want – anything that fits counting repeatedly up to four will work.

If you want to extend this activity, have two tambourines going round the circle at the same time, but this is super ambitious!

Echo!

🐾 Imagine if the dragons called out to the dinosaurs across the mountains, or vice versa. Their voices would echo round the valley. Talk about what the word *echo* means.

🐾 Listen to the ascending scale of C to C played on the CD track 28 with the vocal accompaniment of do ré mi etc. This is called the tonic sol-fa system. Join in singing with the CD.

🐾 Following the scale, you will hear several examples of three sol-fa sounds. After each group of three, there is a pause for you to echo the sounds. Our ability to sing in tune is called *intonation* and children are never too young to start working on good intonation.

Make a class book

Can you make a simple class picture book out of the story 'A Roaring Success'? Or take any character out of the story and create a whole new story for that creature or person.

Percussion echo

🐾 The children should sit in a circle, each with a percussion instrument. Use as many different types as possible. Between you and another adult, you need to have one of every type of the instruments that the children have.

🐾 At any time, either of the adults can pick up any one of their instruments. The children have to keep their eye on both adults. If they see that either one of you is playing 'their' instrument, they must join in until the adult stops, when they must stop too.

🐾 Where possible, trick the children by playing two instruments at once, i.e. sometimes one of the adults might put an instrument down and pick up a different one whilst the other will keep playing the same instrument for a few seconds more. Make your choice of which instrument to play completely random, occasionally repeating one that you only played recently so the children are kept on their toes!

CD Track Listing

1. Song: Block Your Ears! Here It Comes! (vocal)
2. Song: Block Your Ears! Here It Comes! (backing track)
3. Dragon names from the story
4. Song: Dinosaurus Action! (vocal)
5. Song: Dinosaurus Action! (backing track)
6. 'Fossils' from *Carnival Of The Animals* by Saint Saëns
7. Song: Twinkling Stars (vocal)
8. Song: Twinkling Stars (backing track)
9. Dancing smoke and flames
10. Song: The Rain Came Down And Down (vocal)
11. Song: The Rain Came Down And Down (backing track)
12. Song: Hush Little Baby (vocal)
13. Song: Hush Little Baby (backing track)
14. Can you see Baby?
15. Can you see Baby? (backing track)
16. Song: Rock A Bye Baby (vocal)
17. Song: Rock A Bye Baby (backing track)
18. Lullaby by Brahms
19. Sing A Song Of Sixpence
20. Mary, Mary, Quite Contrary
21. Where Oh Where Has My Little Dog Gone?
22. Away In A Manger
23. Lavender's Blue
24. Twinkle Twinkle Little Star
25. Song: A Party In The Dark (vocal)
26. Song: A party In The Dark (backing track)
27. Pass the percussion
28. Echo!

1 2 3 4 5 6 7